Building Em Systems

A beginner's guide to Design Patterns for Great Software

Koso Brown

Contents

Introduction

The Apollo Guidance Computer, created in the 1960s by Dr. Charles Stark Draper at the Massachusetts Institute of Technology for the Apollo Program, was the first contemporary embedded computer system to operate in real-time. The purpose of the Apollo Guidance Computer was to automatically gather data and perform computations essential to the Apollo Command Module and Lunar Module's missions.

To improve embedded system design, the National Engineering Manufacturers Association released a standard for programmable microcontrollers in 1978. By the early 1980s, memory, input, and output system components had been integrated into the same chip as the processor, forming a microcontroller. Intel released the Intel 4004, the first commercially available microprocessor unit, in 1971.

Every element of customers' daily life, from traffic lights and thermostats to credit card readers and cell phones, would eventually have an embedded microcontroller system.

Chapter 1

What is an Embedded System?

A computer hardware and software combination created for a particular purpose is called an embedded system. Embedded systems can operate in a larger system. The systems may have fixed functionality or be programmable. An embedded system may be found in an industrial machine, consumer electronics, agricultural and processing sector devices, cars, medical equipment, cameras, digital watches, home appliances, vending machines, toys, and mobile devices.

Even though they are computer systems, embedded systems can have sophisticated graphical user interfaces (GUIs), as seen in mobile devices, or they can have no UI at all, as in the case of devices made to do a specific purpose. Button, LED (light-emitting diode), and touchscreen sensing are examples of user interfaces. Remote user interfaces are also used by some systems.

Business-to-business (B2B) research firm MarketsandMarkets estimated that the embedded market would reach a valuation of $116.2 billion by 2025. Numerous well-known technology companies, including Apple, IBM, Intel, and Texas Instruments, are among the chip producers for embedded systems. The requirement for chips made for high-level processing, mobile computing, and ongoing investments in artificial intelligence (AI) all contribute to the anticipated growth.

Embedded system examples
Numerous technologies in a variety of industries employ embedded systems. Among the instances are:

- ❖ **Industrial machine.** Both embedded systems and embedded systems themselves may be present in them, such as sensors. Embedded automation systems, which carry out particular monitoring and control tasks, are frequently found in industrial machinery.

4

❖ **Healthcare equipment.** These might have embedded mechanisms, such as control and sensor systems. Industrial and medical machinery alike need to be extremely user-friendly to avoid avoidable machine errors endangering human health. This implies that they frequently have a more sophisticated OS and GUI made for a suitable user interface.

❖ **Smartphones**. These include a variety of embedded systems, such as input/output (I/O) modules for the USB (Universal Serial Bus), cameras, microphones, operating systems (OSes), and GUI software and hardware.

❖ **Automobiles.** Many computers, often as many as 100, or embedded systems, intended to carry out various functions within the vehicle, are a frequent feature of modern cars. While some of these devices carry out simple utilitarian tasks, others entertain or engage the user. Airbags, cruise control, backup sensors, suspension control, and navigation systems are a few embedded systems found in consumer cars.

How to Get Knowledge on Embedded Systems

Having gained a basic understanding of the process of creating an embedded system, let us now move on to discover how to learn embedded systems. This will provide you with a comprehensive understanding of how to begin working with embedded programming and systems.

Knowledge of fundamental electronics

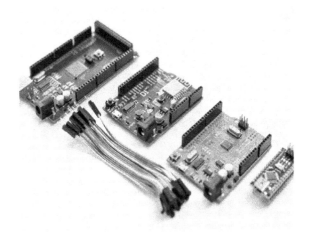

So, learning the fundamentals of electronics should come first. Most likely one of the most crucial points. Since electronics permeates everything we discuss here, learning about electrical components— including how they function and are used—will be crucial to grasping embedded systems. Since electronic components are used throughout the construction of embedded systems, you should learn as much as you can about them. But the first step in getting started is to comprehend the items listed below.

Switching devices: relays

To turn on and off devices using the output of a microcontroller, switching devices and circuits are required. A microcontroller board, such as the Arduino or any other microcontroller, typically outputs only digital signals. There are two possible values for this digital signal: 1 and 0. In terms of electricity, 0 represents the ground voltage and 1 denotes the microcontroller's working voltage. Typically, 0 denotes the negative of the power supply circuit or the GND of the DC supply, while 1 denotes either +3.3 v or +5 v. A physical device, such as a light bulb, cannot be turned on or off with this little voltage. Thus, a transistor receives this power and activates a device known as a relay. The main AC appliances can then be switched using this relay.

LEDs

The most intriguing electrical component in the circuit is probably the LED. Light-emitting Diode (LED) components can emit a particular type of light. It could be yellow, blue, green, or red. LEDs have an extremely long lifespan and require very little voltage—typically 3 volts—to turn ON. LEDs are used in the power indicators of practically all electronic appliances. LEDs are used as the power light in TV remote controls, DVD players, microwaves, and TVs. These days, we have LED TVs, which employ LEDs to backlight the LCD panel within. Additional information regarding LEDs can be found here.

Transistors

Three primary circuit types use transistors.

- ✓ Changing

- ✓ Expansion

- ✓ Generation of oscillation

Transistors are mostly utilized for switching in embedded systems. Transistors have various uses in analog circuits such as oscillators and amplifiers. It is a straightforward three-terminal device that may be purchased as an NPN or PNP transistor. How they conduct and govern electricity is different.

Diodes

In electronics, a diode is a unidirectional switch. A diode's function is to permit current to flow in one direction while obstructing it in the other. Diodes are primarily utilized in circuits that use rectifiers. DC voltage is created by rectifier circuit conversion of AC voltage. Power supplies are made with rectifiers. A diode is employed in many applications where this one-way conduction property is required, aside from rectifiers, such as circuit protection.

Capacitors

A capacitor is a passive electrical component with two leads that was once referred to as a condenser. In an electric circuit, energy is stored in capacitors. There are various kinds of capacitors in use. However, they are always made up of at least two electrical conductor plates that are spaced between by an insulator material, or dielectric. Thin metal films, such as aluminum foil, can serve as the conductors. The capacitor's capacity to store charge is increased by the "nonconducting" dielectric material.

Resistors

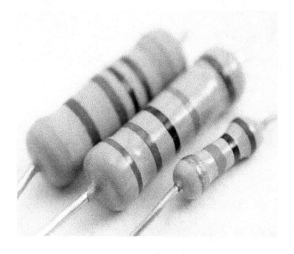

Those tiny small electronic components called resistors are used to block the flow of electric current. A resistor's function is to resist—that is, to oppose—the flow of electricity whenever we attempt to establish a tiny circuit. A resistor's resistance value is always the same. Because resistors are passive parts, they function in the same manner in circuits connected in either direction. We can control the amount of current that flows through a circuit by utilizing resistors

Chapter 2

What's the process of an embedded system?

Embedded refers to the fact that embedded systems are always a component of a whole device. These are tiny, low-cost, low-power computers that are integrated into other electrical or mechanical systems. They typically consist of a processor, memory, communication ports, and a power source. Using a communication protocol, embedded systems use the communication ports to transfer data between the processor and peripheral devices, which are frequently other embedded systems. The CPU uses the basic software that is stored in memory to evaluate this data. Typically, the software is extremely tailored to the purpose of the embedded system.

The processor could be a microcontroller or a microprocessor. Microcontrollers are essentially microprocessors with built-in integrated memory and external ports. Memory and peripherals are not built into microprocessors; instead, they are used by separate integrated circuits. Both are functional, but because microprocessors have less integrated circuitry than microcontrollers, they usually need additional support circuitry. One often uses the term system on a chip (SoC). On a single chip, SoCs have several processors and interfaces. They're frequently applied to embedded systems with large volumes. Application-specific integrated circuits (ASICs) and field-programmable gate arrays (FPGAs) are two examples of SoC kinds.

Real-time operating systems (RTOS) are utilized by embedded systems to interface with hardware in real-time operating environments. At higher levels of chip capability—defined by designers who have increasingly determined that the jobs are tolerant of small fluctuations in reaction time and the systems are generally fast enough—near-real-time techniques are appropriate. Although other OSes, such as Embedded Java and Windows IoT (previously Windows Embedded), have been condensed to run on embedded systems, stripped-down variants of the Linux operating system are frequently used in these situations.

Features of embedded systems

The primary attribute of embedded systems is their task-specific nature. Moreover, embedded systems may include the following features:

- ❖ Often have to do their tasks within a certain amount of time to maintain the smooth operation of the bigger system.
- ❖ Are frequently utilized in Internet of Things (IoT) devices, which are internet-connected gadgets that don't need to be operated by users, for sensing and real-time computation;
- ❖ Either microprocessor- or microcontroller-based, both of which are integrated circuits that provide computing power to the system;
- ❖ Because they are designed for specific activities inside the system rather than a variety of functions, they can be integrated into a bigger system to carry out a particular

purpose;

- ❖ Often comprises firmware, software, and hardware;

The framework of embedded systems

Though they might range in complexity, embedded systems typically comprise three primary components:

- ❖ **Operating system in real-time.** Particularly in smaller-scale embedded systems, these are not always present. By monitoring the software and establishing guidelines as it is being executed, RTOSes control how the system functions.

- ❖ **Firmware and software.** The complexity of software for embedded systems might vary. On the other hand, embedded IoT devices and industrial-grade microcontrollers typically run very basic software with low memory requirements.

- ❖ **Hardware.** The microprocessor and microcontroller are the foundational components of embedded system hardware.

Microprocessors and microcontrollers are closely related. A microprocessor is a central processing unit (CPU) that is coupled with other fundamental computer components including digital signal processors (DSPs) and memory chips. All of those parts are integrated into a single microcontroller chip.

A basic embedded system's hardware would include the following components:

- ✓ Actuators select the proper output by comparing the actual output with the output stored in memory.
- ✓ Digital-to-analog (D-A) converters transform the processor's digital data into analog data.
- ✓ Digital signals are processed by processors and then stored in memory.
- ✓ An analog electrical signal is converted to a digital one using analog-to-digital (A-D) converters.
- ✓ Sensors generate an electrical signal from physical sense data.

The sensor receives input from the outside world, converters make it legible for the CPU, and the processor then converts that data into output that the embedded system may use.

Embedded system types

A few fundamental types of embedded systems exist, with varying functional needs. They are as follows:

❖ **Real-time embedded systems** provide the needed result within a predetermined window of time. Since they are in charge of time-sensitive duties, they are frequently employed in the industrial, military, and medical sectors. An illustration of this would be a traffic control system.

❖ **Independent embedded systems** lack dependence on a host system. Just like every other embedded system, they carry out a certain function. Unlike other embedded systems, though, they are not always a part of a host system. An MP3 player or calculator are

21

two examples of this.

❖ **Embedded networks** are wired into a network to supply output to other systems. Point of sale (POS) systems and home security systems are two examples.

❖ **Mobile embedded systems** are compact systems made to be carried around. Take digital cameras as an illustration.

Another way to classify embedded systems is based on their performance needs: a larger microcontroller

❖ **Advanced-level embedded systems** frequently employ many algorithms, which increases the complexity of the hardware and software and calls for the usage of programmable logic arrays, configurable processors, and/or more complicated software.

❖ **Embedded systems on a medium scale** utilize a larger microcontroller (16–32 bits) and connect microcontrollers frequently.

❖ **Small-scale embedded systems** frequently make use of only an 8-bit microcontroller.

Several common software architectures for embedded systems are required as these systems expand and take on greater complexity. Among them are:

❖ **Preemptive multitasking or multithreading** has synchronization and job-switching techniques, and it is frequently used in conjunction with an RTOS.

❖ **Cooperative multitasking** is essentially an application programming interface (API) that has a basic control loop.

❖ **Interrupt controlled systems** possess a primary loop and a secondary loop. Tasks are initiated when loop disruptions occur.

❖ **Simple control loops** are called subroutines, which are used in embedded programming or hardware to control a particular component.

Chapter 3

Debugging Embedded Systems

Debugging is one area where embedded systems diverge from other larger-scale computers' operating systems and development environments. While working with desktop computer environments, developers typically have computers that can run both the code they are developing and independent debugger software that can monitor the embedded system; this is not always the case, though.

Certain programming languages are efficient enough to operate on microcontrollers, allowing for on-chip, basic interactive debugging. Furthermore, a JTAG or comparable debugging interface can be used to control CPU debuggers on CPUs, which in turn controls program execution.

However, programmers frequently require tools that connect an independent debugging system via a serial or other connection to the target machine. In this example, debugging software on a desktop computer is analogous to the programmer seeing the source code on the screen of a general-purpose computer. Alternatively, and more commonly, software can be used to simulate the physical chip on a PC. In essence, this enables debugging the software's performance as though it were operating on a real, physical chip.

In general, testing and debugging of embedded systems have gained increased attention because many devices that use embedded controls are intended for use, particularly in scenarios where dependability and safety are of utmost importance.

The Embedded Design

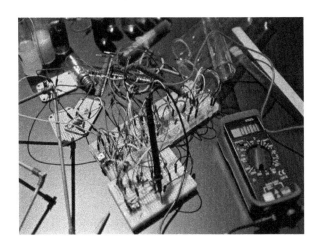

An embedded design is quite easy to construct. All that will be included is the microcontroller unit, which will handle the tasks of driving the display, reading sensors, and switching output devices (relays). The controller's software controls how the device reads the temperature sensor, outputs the value, and performs all of these functions. Unlike typical analog or digital circuits, an embedded controller cannot operate directly. Rather, an embedded microcontroller requires a program to be stored in its memory that will handle device control. An IC that can be reconfigured is the microcontroller.

The microcontroller's pins are capable of doing many tasks such as input, output, analog input, and more. The behavior of the microcontroller's pins can vary depending on the software that has been written. Understanding microcontroller architecture is necessary to become proficient in microcontroller coding. We can begin developing the programs for the microcontroller once we have thoroughly studied its architecture. However, many people are unable to directly plunge into embedded systems due to this significant constraint. The Arduino board enters the scene at this point. We don't need to understand anything about the underlying hardware—referred to as the microcontroller board—to program an Arduino board. Soon, we'll go into more detail on the Arduino board.

How is an embedded system constructed?
Thus, an embedded system is constructed with this kind of microcontroller at its core. All of the relevant input and output devices are either directly interfaced with the microcontroller in an embedded system or connected to it through a driver circuit. The components depicted in the diagram below may comprise all or some of an embedded system, depending on the specific application.

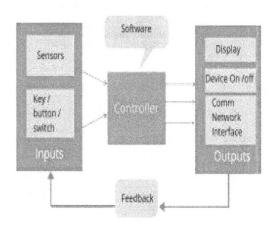

Topology of Embedded System

What are the different components of Embedded Systems?

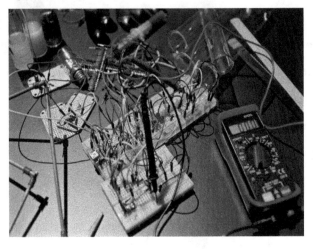

Just glance at the block diagram up top. This embedded system block diagram is quite basic. Well, it truly is simple, I promise. The block diagram provides an overview of an embedded system and conceals nearly all of its complexity. Three key components of the embedded system are displayed in the embedded systems block diagram.

A **controller** is an embedded system's central component. It is the responsibility of a controller to process inputs and produce outputs. The internal controller of a temperature controller is responsible for reading the switches and the temperature value. Next, control output devices by comparing the temperature value with a predetermined point. All of these functions are not available to controllers out of the box; instead, software must reside inside each controller to perform these functions. Software programming for embedded devices becomes more in demand as a result.

Among the most often utilized controllers in embedded systems are

- ✓ System on Chip (SoC)

- ✓ Microprocessor

- ✓ PLDs (FPGA / CPLD)

✓ Microcontroller

Outputs This is the only reason any system is designed. We must provide results. Typically, a range of driver circuits that can produce output action are used to generate outputs. If microcontrollers are utilized, their output can only produce modest signals. either +3.3v or +5v as the output voltages. Since these voltages are so low that they are unable to directly drive any output device, we require an output driver to turn on and off devices. The examples of embedded system outputs below, together with the corresponding drivers,

✓ Data visualization (LCD / LED screen interfacing)
✓ Data transmission via the Internet for remote observation (Wi-Fi interface)
✓ Fan on/off (thyristor driver, resistor, or relay)
✓ SMS Transmission (GSM Module)
✓ motors that rotate at different speeds (motor driver)
✓ Buzzer On-off and sound generation (no

driver)

- ✓ devices that turn on and off. (relay driver plus transistor)
- ✓ LED On / Off (No Driver)

Inputs can typically originate from sensors or switches. Switches will be used as inputs in the temperature controller example to receive both the temperature sensor and the setpoint. Similar to this, a moisture level sensor will be a part of a plant watering system.

Chapter 4

What role does Arduino play in embedded systems?

Understanding the controller is typically the area of study that receives the greatest attention in an embedded system. Developing embedded systems requires a deep understanding of the microcontrollers that are utilized in the system, including how to write programs for them and understand all of their instructions. Each microcontroller has one or more of the following features, which are necessary for correctly programming embedded systems.

- ✓ RAM, Flash, and EEPROM memory
- ✓ Interrupts (to speed up processing and make difficult programming problems easier to solve)
- ✓ Protocols interfacing (I2C / SPI)
- ✓ Converter from Digital to Analog
- ✓ Serial Ports
- ✓ Counters and timers
- ✓ Ports for input and output

An all-in-one microcontroller chip contains all of these functions. The microcontroller developer has to come up with a novel method of configuring the microcontroller to employ any of these functionalities.

- ❖ Every microcontroller, which can do various tasks like reading and writing data from memory, input-output ports, and all of the controller's registers, has its own set of instructions.

35

❖ Second, the microcontroller has a large number of unique function registers. The microcontroller may include one or more Special Function registers for each functionality.

❖ A study of microcontroller architecture is the examination of the instruction set and the arrangement of every internal register taken together.

Therefore, every embedded systems developer needs to have a solid grasp of both the inputs and outputs that are to be used, as well as the architecture of the microcontroller. This is often taught to students studying electronics and computer engineering as part of their coursework; anyone else who is interested in excelling in microcontroller studies must do independent research on the subject. It is imperative to possess a thorough understanding of microcontroller architecture.

However,

What about those enthusiasts or creatives who wish to create embedded systems but are ignorant of microcontrollers?

In 2005, Arduino boards were introduced in Italy as a solution for individuals much like them who wish to start building systems more quickly and smoothly without having to study architecture. You may read about the lengthy history of Arduino boards here. Arduino exists only to make it easier for non-techies to begin creating embedded system hobby projects.

However, millions of individuals, including seasoned professionals, began adopting the Arduino system over time because of its open-source nature for very basic reasons.

- ✓ It is inexpensive.
- ✓ Open-source and cost-free
- ✓ It is possible to prototype quickly.

✓ Almost all interfaces have a large number of clean libraries accessible.

However, what exactly is Arduino?

The Arduino board is a functioning microcontroller-based board. To utilize Arduino, you don't have to learn about microcontroller architecture. It is sufficient to be able to read the board and comprehend simple English to begin programming an Arduino. You may see a different tutorial I wrote about it here.

Chapter 5

Embedded systems' purpose.

Embedded systems are designed to manage a particular task inside a device. Although more advanced embedded systems are capable of controlling whole operating systems, they are often only intended to carry out this task regularly.

Even while some more sophisticated embedded systems are capable of carrying out several activities, these are still comparatively easy tasks that don't demand a lot of computing capacity.

One important feature of embedded systems is that they are typically not programmable, meaning that once configured to carry out a certain task, they function dependably and don't require tampering. On some embedded systems devices, however, it is possible to upgrade the software, which allows for the improvement of programmed capabilities.

The single-purpose architecture and programming of

embedded systems make them dependable electronic components that are very simple to integrate into a device and require little upkeep. Although they are an important feature of many devices that require interaction only to function, such as domestic appliances, they are also a crucial component of many systems since they are highly unlikely to malfunction and do not require reprogramming.

Types of Embedded Systems

Although the majority of these parts have fairly similar designs and functions, there are several distinct types of embedded systems with unique features that call for varying degrees of expertise to install and develop. Embedded systems that fall into more than one of these categories are available, including independent and mobile embedded systems.

Independent Embedded system

Described as autonomous or stand-alone, an embedded system functions independently and doesn't need a host system, such as a computer, to do so. It does not require a connection to any other network or system to gather input data, process it, and carry out the necessary operation. Microwaves and other appliances that measure temperature are common examples.

Embedded Network System

A machine or device that is linked to a network and outputs data to other systems is said to be an embedded network system. They are commonly seen in home security systems where a smaller device is needed to carry out a basic task or react to a particular input, and then it needs to communicate with a larger, more intricate system that is connected by a network.

Mobile Embedded System

Any embedded system employed in a compact, portable device is referred to as a mobile embedded system. They are present in digital cameras, watches, music players, and cell phones in addition to other devices. They are typically rather basic and need little power and memory.

Embedded system software components

Embedded system software is particularly created for a single type of device, and its goals are much narrower than those of computer software, which may be loaded on numerous devices to achieve the same goal. The embedded systems' software consists of the following:

Debugging

Lastly, a software tool for testing and debugging is the

debugger. It is in charge of going over the code, eliminating bugs and other mistakes, and emphasizing the precise places where they happened. Debuggers enable programmers to quickly fix issues.

Editor for links

Typically, software code is written in short segments and modules. The component that takes one or more object files and integrates them to create a single executable code is called a link editor, or "linker."

Emulator

This part operates the embedded system in a simulation environment and makes it act like a real-life system. In short, it helps guarantee optimal written code performance by simulating software performance. To get a sense of how the code will run in real-time, utilize the emulator.

Assembler

This differs slightly from the procedure that a compiler uses. Written code is translated straight into machine language by the compiler. Conversely, the assembler translates source code into object code first, and then object code into machine language.

When an application is built using assembly language as the programming language, the assembler is utilized. For additional processing, the assembly language program is converted to HEX code. The programmer is used to write the program on the chip after the code has been written.

Text Editor

The first piece of software required to construct an embedded system is a text editor. Writing source code in the C and C++ programming languages is done with this editor and then saved as a text file.

Compiler

Creating an executable program is the main duty of this component. The machine needs to comprehend the code once it has been prepared in the text editor.

The compiler assists in this by converting the written code into low-level machine language. Machine code, assembly language, and object code are a few examples of low-level languages.

Applications of Embedded Systems

Several technologies, such as machine-to-machine (M2M) devices and the Internet of Things (IoT), depend heavily on embedded systems. These days, almost all smart devices make use of this adaptable technology in one way or another.

Here are a few examples of embedded system uses in the real world:

Self-serve terminals

Interactive self-service kiosks provide consumers with services and information in settings where it is impractical for a human employee to be present. Imagine a ticket office serving patrons of a 2 a.m. showing at a largely deserted theater. There are many different types of self-service kiosks, such as snack vending machines and filling stations equipped with self-checkout systems. Airports, department stores, healthcare facilities, public buildings, and several more places have these kiosks. The processing power needed for these kiosks to give clients an interactive experience is provided by embedded systems.

Facilities for charging electric vehicles

Electric power is supplied via electric car charging stations to recharge the batteries of linked electric automobiles. Among the many tasks performed by embedded systems in charging stations include alerting technicians to impending maintenance needs, automatically highlighting technical concerns, and providing processing power for visual displays.

Manufacturing

Robots are used in many procedures in factories today that call for high-precision precision work, hazardous work environments, or both. Robots used in typical automated tasks must be equipped with sensors, actuators, and software that enable them to "perceive" their surroundings and produce the necessary results effectively and safely. To do this, robots are outfitted with embedded systems that connect them to a variety of subsystems.

Without these embedded systems, plant automation robots would have to rely on external computing and control systems. Increased safety concerns may result from connectivity problems or delays in human response. To make equipment safer, more effective, and wiser, plant automation systems are integrating embedded systems with artificial intelligence and machine learning more and more as Industry 4.0 becomes a reality.

These solutions, for example, enable robots to automatically detect and eliminate production flaws before the human eye can notice them. Applications for factory robots with embedded systems include quality control and assembly.

Automated Teller Machines

Globally employed in the banking industry, automated teller machines (ATMs) are sizable computerized electronic devices. An ATM uses a network connection to communicate with the host bank computer during a transaction. The information processed during the transaction is stored by the bank computer, which also checks the data entered. Simultaneously, the ATM displays transaction data from the bank computer and processes user inputs from the field using embedded devices.

Home Entertainment

Televisions and other entertainment devices are commonplace in households all around the world. When it comes to reading inputs from ports like the antenna, DisplayPort, HDMI, and Ethernet, embedded systems are essential. In addition, remote controls send out infrared signals that televisions can read. Even the operating system on smart televisions supports streaming media and the internet. These tasks are critical to embedded systems, which are becoming more and more popular as new methods for improving the intelligence of home entertainment are found.

Trackers for Fitness

Fitness trackers are wearable gadgets that track health indicators and activities including walking, jogging, and sleeping. They have grown in popularity. These gadgets use embedded systems to gather information on body temperature, heart rate, and number of steps taken. Using a wide area network (WAN) like LTE or GPRS, this data is sent to servers.

Automated fare collection

Passengers on public transit can pay their fares online or through automated equipment without speaking to a human agent thanks to automated fare collection methods. The ecosystem for automatic transit fare collection includes ticketing machines, ticket and card checking machines, automatic gate machines, and regular travelers' smart and magnetic stripe cards. To maintain the mechanism's functionality and allow them to communicate with one another, all of these components have embedded systems.

Automotive

In automobile applications, embedded systems improve user experience and overall safety. Adaptive speed control, pedestrian detection, auto breakdown warning, merging assistance, airbag deployment, anti-lock brake systems, and in-car entertainment systems are some prominent instances of embedded systems in operation.

Medical Equipment

Embedded medical devices are state-of-the-art tools used for patients who need continuous monitoring. For example, embedded sensors collect health information from implants, heart rate, and pulse rate. After that, this data is sent to a private cloud, where a medical expert can manually review it or an alarm system can review it automatically.

GPS

To provide a global navigation system, the global positioning system (GPS) synchronizes location, velocity, and time data using satellites and receivers. GPS systems are frequently seen in cars and portable electronics. To utilize the global positioning system, all "receivers" (i.e., devices that receive GPS data) are integrated with embedded systems.

Conclusion

Embedded devices can be found in everything from printers and routers to EV charging stations, elevators, and point-of-sale machines. To put it simply, they are present everywhere in the modern world. Despite their diminutive size, they are robust, designed with purpose, and have a quick processing speed. They propel apps' superior real-time performance. Moreover, embedded systems are growing more capable and intelligent, which expands their use in edge computing, the Internet of Things, graphics rendering, and other areas.

Embedded systems are tiny computers that are included in bigger systems to carry out particular functions like data processing and graphics. They are extensively utilized in the modern world and have a big impact on how we go about our daily lives, including how we pass the time, commute, conduct business, and enjoy ourselves.